SCHOLASTIC
News
Nonfiction Readers

High Point Media Center

Mercury

by
Christine Taylor-Butler

Children's Press®
A Division of Scholastic Inc.
New York Toronto London Auckland Sydney
Mexico City New Delhi Hong Kong
Danbury, Connecticut

These content vocabulary word builders
are for grades 1-2.

Consultant: Daniel D. Kelson, Ph.D.
Carnegie Observatories
Pasadena, CA

Curriculum Specialist: Linda Bullock

Photo Credits:

Photographs © 2005: Corbis Images: 2, 5 top right, 17 (Sergi Remezov/Reuters), 1, 19; Finley Holiday Film: back cover; NASA: 5 top left, 15 top, 15 bottom; Photo Researchers, NY: 11 (Chris Butler), 4 top, 13 (Lynette Cook), 4 bottom right (Ted Kinsman), 5 bottom left (David Nunuk/SPL), cover, 4 bottom left, 7, 23 (U.S. Geological Survey/SPL), 5 bottom right, 9 (Detlev van Ravenswaay); PhotoDisc/Getty Images via SODA: 23 left.

Book Design: Simonsays Design!

Library of Congress Cataloging-in-Publication Data

Taylor-Butler, Christine.
    Mercury / by Christine Taylor-Butler.
        p. cm. — (Scholastic news nonfiction readers)
    Includes bibliographical references and index.
    ISBN 0-516-24917-7 (lib. bdg.)
    1. Mercury (Planet)—Juvenile literature. I. Title. II. Series.
    QB611.T39 2005
    523.41—dc22
                                2005002327

1 2 3 4 5 6 7 8 9 10 R 14 13 12 11 10 09 08 07 06 05

CONTENTS

WORD HUNT

Look for these words as you read. They will be in **bold**.

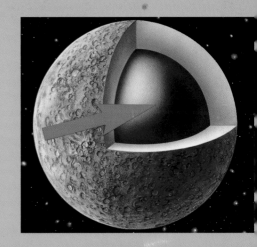

core
(kor)

Mercury
(**muhr**-kyur-ree)

meteorite
(**mee**-tee-ur-ite)

crater
(**kray**-tur)

float
(floht)

moon
(moon)

solar system
(**soh**-lur **siss**-t

9

Mercury!

Can you sing on **Mercury**?

No. You cannot sing on Mercury.

You can't even breathe. Mercury has no air.

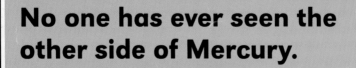

No one has ever seen the other side of Mercury.

Mercury is one of the smallest planets in the **solar system**.

Only Pluto is smaller than Mercury.

Mercury is the planet closest to the Sun.

Pluto

Sun

Mercury

The side of the planet that faces the Sun is boiling hot.

The side that faces away from the Sun is freezing cold.

Mercury is only 36 million miles from the Sun.

Mercury is made mostly of iron.

It has a very big **core** for such a little planet.

Scientists think the core is made of liquid iron.

core

crust

13

Mercury looks like Earth's **moon**.

Mercury and the Moon both have many **craters**.

The craters were made millions of years ago.

Some of the craters were made when **meteorites** hit Mercury and the Moon.

crater on
Mercury

crater on
Earth's moon

Gravity on Mercury is different than gravity on Earth.

Gravity is the pull between two objects.

You would weigh less on Mercury than on Earth.

You would **float**!

This astronaut practices floating.

Scientists know some facts about Mercury because of Mariner 10.

Mariner 10 is a space probe.

A space probe does not carry people.

You cannot go to Mercury. Scientists are glad that a space probe can!

Mariner 10

19

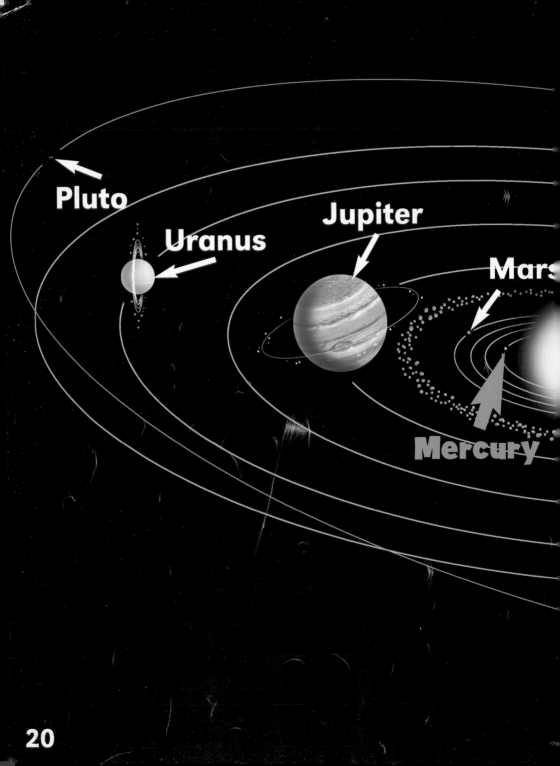

Pluto

Uranus

Jupiter

Mars

Mercury

MERCURY

IN OUR SOLAR SYSTEM

Sun

Venus

Earth

Saturn

Neptune

YOUR NEW WORDS

core (kor) the inside of a planet

crater (**kray**-tur) a dent or hole in a planet

float (floht) to rest on water or air

Mercury (**muhr**-kyur-ree) a planet named after the Roman messenger of the gods

meteorite (**mee**-tee-ur-ite) a rock made of metal and stone that comes from outer space and lands on Earth

moon (moon) an object that circles a planet

solar system (**soh**-lur **siss**-tuhm) the group of planets, moons, and other things that travel around the Sun

Earth and Mercury

A year is how long it takes a planet to go around the Sun.

 Earth's year =365 days

 Mercury's year =88 Earth days

A day is how long it takes a planet to turn one time.

 Earth's day = 24 hours

 Mercury's day = 1,408 Earth hours

A moon is an object that circles a planet.

Earth has 1 moon

Mercury has no moons

Did you know that the Sun can rise on Mercury two times in one day?

INDEX

FIND OUT MORE
Book:
Children's Atlas of the Universe
By Robert Burnham
Reader's Digest Children's Publishing, Inc., 2000

Website:
Solar System Exploration
http://sse.jpl.nasa.gov/planets

MEET THE AUTHOR:

Christine Taylor-Butler is the author of more than 20 books for children. She holds a degree in Engineering from M.I.T. She lives in Kansas City with her family, where they have a telescope for searching the skies.